GOALIE

T0349066

FIRST POETS SERIES 26

Canada Council
for the Arts

Conseil des Arts
du Canada

ONTARIO ARTS COUNCIL
CONSEIL DES ARTS DE L'ONTARIO

an Ontario government agency
un organisme du gouvernement de l'Ont

Ontario

Canada

Guernica Editions Inc. acknowledges the support of the Canada Council
for the Arts and the Ontario Arts Council. The Ontario Arts Council
is an agency of the Government of Ontario.

We acknowledge the financial support of the Government of Canada.

BEN VON JAGOW

GOALIE

GUERNICA
EDITIONS

TORONTO – CHICAGO – BUFFALO – LANCASTER (U.K.)

2025

Guernica Founder: Antonio D'Alfonso

Michael Mirolla, general editor
Elana Wolff, editor
Cover design: Ben von Jagow & Ajax Olson
Interior design: Errol F. Richardson

Guernica Editions Inc.
1241 Marble Rock Rd., Gananoque, ON K7G 2V4
2250 Military Road, Tonawanda, N.Y. 14150-6000 U.S.A.
www.guernicaeditions.com

Distributors:
Independent Publishers Group (IPG)
600 North Pulaski Road, Chicago IL 60624
University of Toronto Press Distribution (UTP)
5201 Dufferin Street, Toronto (ON), Canada M3H 5T8

First edition.
Printed in Canada.

Legal Deposit—First Quarter
Library of Congress Catalog Card Number: 2024946707
Library and Archives Canada Cataloguing in Publication
Title: Goalie / Ben von Jagow.
Names: Von Jagow, Ben, author.
Series: First poets series (Toronto, Ont.) ; 26.
Description: Series statement: First poets series ; 26
Identifiers: Canadiana 20240460707 | ISBN 9781771839488 (softcover)
Subjects: LCGFT: Sports poetry. | LCGFT: Poetry.
Classification: LCC PS8643.O534 G63 2025 | DDC C811/.6—dc23

For 4.

Contents

"So enticing, deep dark seas. It's so easy to drown in the dream."
—Sturgill Simpson

The Rink

It started with a single tarp, fifteen by twenty.
In those days it was just my neighbour, Leif.
No boards, not even a net, he fired shots into

the snowbank. The rink blossomed by season.
Leif unfolding more and more canvas till the
man in the blue vest shook his head. *Sorry.*

From my bedroom window, I watched him stitch
the tarps together. Seven rolls of duct tape.
He filled it with water and waited.

Later that week, temperatures dropped.
Leif the first on the ice, a Saturday morning.
Sunshine and tentative cuts, a lone puck sliding.

Following night, the season opener. Leif and his buddies.
Through that same bedroom window, I listened. Carved ice,
chirrups, pucks on plywood. Sounds that spoke worlds.

Leif missed days on the rink that season, his life beginning
to shift. I'd hear his car pull out in the morning and creep
back late at night, his headlights sweeping across my wall,

the framed poster of Potvin, a Rushmore of bobbleheads.
He drove out west the following winter and willed me
his tricks. Carrying the kettle outside, defrosting the spigot,

listening for the rush of water. With an arthritic hose and
a painter's stroke, I learned to resurrect a body scarred.
Frozen mist beneath floodlights. Prisms of colour. Beauty

in the infinite. In summer, I combed that same space with
my mower. Autumn, I raked leaves. Taming nature
through seasons. The relentless onslaught of water and earth.

Those nights, my breath rose to nowhere. A slow drip
from the nozzle freezing my gloved fingers. A delicate sheen
reflecting moonlight, floodlights, the black space above.

Afterward, hose coiled in the basement, skates laced.
Something about the way that ice glimmered after a flood.
Like a blank page, untainted and pure. Awaiting characters

and a story scrawled in blades.

Show Stoppers

School book fair, handful of toonies,
warm and metallic. I bought the poster,
stuck it to my wall with clear hockey tape.
Show Stoppers, the poster read. It boasted the big four:
Roy, Brodeur, Cujo, Hasek. The goalie pantheon.
From first glance, you saw freedom, all the intricacies
the position afforded. A uniqueness
unmatched in sport.
The league's four best, and you'd be hard pressed to find
a similarity amongst them.
Numbers, tape jobs, equipment, all different.
But what catches the eye are the stances. No two alike.
Hasek is coiled, crouched like a feline waiting to pounce.
Roy stands tall, like a bear on its hind legs.
Brodeur's moving, always moving.
Cujo's gaze extends beyond the puck. Like an oracle,
he's tracking plays as they develop.
Show Stoppers.
Hung above my bed
in prime poster real estate.
I used to lie backwards, socked feet against the wall, and search
those frozen stances for answers.
Years later, rash decision, I would pull that poster down.
It claimed four penny-sized paint chips. Crisper thin.
That might've told me something about young dreams.
They cling fiercely.
I hung a map there instead, which covers the chips
in the wall, but offers little in terms of inspiration.
A map is a fine thing. Detailed. Objective.
But there's no room for discovery.
Every map is an imitation. A copy of a pre-existing map.
My geography is killer. I know the capitals of all ten provinces,
the three territories, where rivers run.
Sometimes I look up expecting caged faces, and feel loss.

I tried moving my idols to the spot above the dresser;
but the same tape that claimed the paint also tore the poster.
It's still here somewhere. I can't bear to bin it.
Like spoiled art, it adorns no wall.
There's a rip through Roy. One of Hasek's legs is missing.
But it serves as a reminder.
Sometimes, things are better left untouched.
When priorities shift, there can only be damage.

The Church of Saturday Saints

A Cujo bobblehead
atop the TV like a crucifix
live on Saturday night.

A mangy grey tennis ball
striking the far wall
like a mantra.

The opening brass riff
to Hockey Night in Canada.
Please rise for our national anthem.

An Alexander Mogilny
ministick with the illegal
stovetop curve.

A Cooper baseball glove,
a pair of old pillow pads,
a carpeted crease.

Bunny ears beamed the greats
directly into your living room.
Miracles broadcasted on CBC.

Saturday night, God took the form
of a stick paddle, a lunging glove.
Screens from BC to Newfoundland.

Brodeur the trailblazer, Hasek the acrobat,
then the ten o'clock game,
Salo and Turek, the battle of Alberta.

The silver bowl tips before the third,
bouncing kernels punctuate the night.
Ron MacLean talks but goes unheard.

The following morning
Father Matthew's voice,
a drone from the pulpit.

I lip-sync with the choir,
so they can't tell I'm tired
from a night full of worship.

At the Stittsville Dance

Tonight, in darkness, strobe, and colour
I'm gonna wiggle, boogie, and cha-cha
real smooth with the uncaged youth.
My pucca shells are gonna rock the wave
of my Vince Carter J I'll be jumping so much.
Tonight, I might just work up the courage
to ask Chris McDonald to ask Leah Hanley
to ask Dani Simard to slow dance. But hey,
that's songs away. Right now, me and ninety
other pre-pubescent squirts from school
are gonna hop in sync to the Hamsterdance.
We're gonna Crank Dat, Lean Back, and Cotton
Eye Joe till it's time we G2G. Oh, we'll pay our
$5 admission fee (plus pizza and pop) without
grumble because that's the price one pays
for freedom (that's the price one's parents pay).
Tonight, me and the fellas are gonna sneak
glances at the girls from class. Coloured lights
will illuminate their metal braces, sweaty faces,
silly bandz, and secrets. We'll groove in their
orbit, our Axe clouds clashing with their
Shoppers perfume samples. We'll watch them
jig, like giraffes, limbs flailing, awkward
and carefree. Tonight, we're gonna dance
with karate kick enthusiasm. We'll Y, M, C, and
Ayyyy Macarena till the caged clock ticks ten,
the lights turn on, and the chaperones shoo us
out into the night, where Chris' Mom's Malibu
will be parked by the softball diamond, waiting.

No Tourney Too Far

Piled into the bus, parents and players alike,
a nervous chatter permeating the lone aisle.
Leaving the arena parking lot
like embarking on a new world.

By Petawawa the steam had settled.
Someone put on a movie, Superbad,
which lasted all of fifteen minutes
before Doug's dad stork-stepped
his way to the front and hit eject.

I booed with the rest of my team,
relieved with the knowledge that
if it hadn't been him, it would've
been my own mother. Doug shrank.
Far too early in this long journey
for social manslaughter.

Time lulled the buzz till it was a soda gone flat.
Nothing to do but watch the same scratched discs
we had at home. *Miracle, Mighty Ducks 2 & 3, Slapshot.*
If a movie froze, no one jeered. We just nodded,
resignedly, as though this were our lot in life.

After Sudbury, there was nothing. Just trees and lakes.
Trees and lakes. An enormous void. Filled with nothing
but trees and lakes.

Someone tied Luke into a sweatshirt. We barricaded Big Nick
in the bathroom. Those were a swell couple of minutes.

Large glass windows revealed nothing.
No landmarks, barns, or billboards,
we constructed our own green signs:

Highway 17, Welcome to Purgatory

That ride taught us more about our country's size
than any map tacked to the classroom wall.

Tedium. Timelessness. Then, out of nowhere, entity.

I want to say we noticed the lights first,
that Thunder Bay glowed like a lonely Arctic outpost.
That we, sixteen adolescent boys, abandoned our games,
plucked headphones, shook off sleep, and pressed our foreheads
against the cold, vibrating glass to take it all in.
But it was the downshifting of gears, the deceleration,
and the gentle slope of the off-ramp that signalled our arrival.
Our first turn in fifteen hours.

We pulled into the hotel and stormed the lobby like bees,
our energy strumming a discord with the after-dinner crowd.
The day was unwinding, and here we were, convicts turned loose.
We ran the halls like banshees, atoning for lost hours.
Hammer-fisting doors, mosh-pitting in the elevator, flinging
towels from the roof. Sixteen little hoodlums running amok.
Marco the manager eventually set us straight with an ultimatum.
The choice became simple when Coach got involved.
His jaw clenched, that single vein in his forehead throbbing,
the one we knew too well.
They won't make a peep, he said to Marco, his eyes on us.
We believed him.

The following morning, breakfast, the bus puffing fumes out front.
A Canadian day. Sunshine and a wind so cold it froze your
nostrils.

The same bus with the same mess,
but a new sense of purpose.
A shorter journey.

In the arena, mayhem.
Teams from all over.
Cards, programs, pins.

Prairie boys with farm shoulders.
French Canadians with slick accents and nasty toe-drags.
Steeltown kids, East-Coasters, Yanks.

Sixteen kids from the suburbs,
bags slung over our shoulders—
plus the weight of the world.

In due time those games would mean little.
Medals, worn proudly, would go from chest to mantle,
mantle to basement.
Scores would blend, individual plays all but disappear.

What we're apt to remember, years from now, may not be much.
Memory is tricky like that.
It may cling to a drill in practice, the flimsy architecture
of an old rink, or something yelled from the bench.
It might preserve helmets and gloves, the time Drew hit a stick
into the stands, or the way Fergie could taunt an entire team
with only a shift in his voice.
But most likely it will cling to those moments off the ice.
Those dressing room moments. Rooster's dad telling him to
Get the fuck in gear. Rooster winking, putting his pants back on,
his dad leaving the rink.
Running—really running—down a long hotel hallway in socked feet.
Or something from that bus. Fifteen hours reduced
to a single fleeting feeling,
of anticipation, of boredom, of anguish and serenity,
losing and winning, meshed into one.

Teamplay

Chicken fights and continental breakfasts.
Manhunt and ministicks.
In those long hotel halls, we ran.
Hockey cards and Homer slippers.
Ding-dong and ditch.
Shampoos pocketed just because.
We annexed the boardroom. Sullied the board.
Never were bored.
Teammates scouring every stairwell
till curfew.
Till that alarm rang
and those blinking red numbers
told you it was time.
A yawn chain in the dressing room,
nudges, and whose dad ordered PPV.
Cam, the other goalie, pencilled in
for the second and semis.
I've got one and three.
I watch him work the gate, crack jokes.
And when that first one squeaks by me, I swear
that bench just moves further away.

Time Is Like

Final sixty and we're up by one.
The clock like a sun
eclipsed in the second,
fierce in the third,
a stillness before the set.

Rousselle's on the ice, imposing
the presence of an older brother
and Rowe might be able to pot one
in the empty net
if someone can get him the puck.

The numbers on the board
like that last bit of sauce
caught in the bottle.

*

Einstein showed the world that time
does not follow a tick-tock rhythm
but any kid could've told you that.

Minutes stretch in the classroom, a rubber band
pulled wide.
Same goes for the dentist. Time and body suspended
in an upturned chair.
But time's bend is cruellest in the final minute.

*

To succeed in this sport is to disassociate
time from objective.
Many a goalie falters in those final seconds
catering to two birds.
Clock. Puck. Only one has the power
to change the score.

      *

Time is not absolute.
Beyond the blue line, it disappears
like water on a hot dock.

In the crease, it hangs still,
like a damp towel.

Like water.
Time is like water.

Of all the sports
in all the world
only in the arena
has some cruel soul
managed to freeze it.

L'entraineur

The position permitted freedom, I learned that from Hasek.
No one got on your case so long as the puck stayed out.

The jump to Midget was a spring dive.
Players changing from Intermediate to Senior sticks,
lightweight composites with 100 Flex—
the shots came quicker.
I wanted time to acclimatize but the team panicked,
brought in a guy from across the river to polish my edges.

Coach Richard, pronounced like the Rocket,
apparently had quite the stint in the Q, the Nordiques eyeing him,
then one of his teammates wipes a blade, hurls the slush
at his goalie and takes out an eye. No more NHL.
A lifetime of pucks to the body and what does him in
is a bit of melted snow, some post-practice shenanigans.
Christ, no wonder he was so bitter.

Rapid-fire tirades, emotional bruises,
the scene with the dumbbell and the tape,
the whole team watching.
Gardes ton baton sur la glace!

I feared him, I loathed him
but slowly, my game took shape.

All those hours together,
the two of us alone in the crease, face to cage.
Milky sweat beads clinging to the temple,
a body cleansing the day's smoke.

And when I no longer could bear to listen
to the geometry of angles, the merits of the T-push
and when to use the shuffle, I'd turn my eyes
to the other end of the rink
and watch my teammates
fire shot after shot into the empty net.

Pont du Portage

Summer nights we dared cross that bridge,
lured by birds who trilled differently,
lenient bouncers, stories to share come fall.

More than once, we spilled from those clubs,
jaws clenched, itching, not knowing what rule
we were breaking but knowing it was dire.

Jesse fled, Simpson got jumped, and there were
rumours, though I don't know how true,
about one of the 94's doing something in an alley

with a team from the O. Probably bullshit. But hey,
you either chased stories or were chased home.
Pressed into the backseat of someone's mom's car,

ear to the cold glass, a lingering taste of whiskey sours,
the sign could read *Portage Bridge* or *Pont du Portage*,
depending on which way you faced.

Prescient

On those nights the game made sense.
My pace in sync with the march of time,
the puck adhering to a traceable logic.

On those nights I played for smiles
and pad taps. I pushed the boundaries
of my reputation. I instilled belief.

On those nights I was a river
fluid, consistent,
an effortless momentum.

Even if one did squeak past,
the iron sang. A goalie's best friend,
a mysterious universe.

On those nights, I tracked plays
like constellations.
My eyes could sequence the stars.

On those nights, I silenced the voice,
conquered the current
and rode in the surf.

On those nights, I was

The Dream Chaser

Dreams blossom at dawn,
bobbing branches scatter beams of sunlight,
the bed like a stick of warm butter. To slip back into
a sleep so delicious as easy as letting go.

Dreams are sowed in the morning.
Feet on the cold floor,
shaking out night's warmth,
exchanged for heat in a cup, a clear mind.

The alarm is recognized more so than heard—
like the next key
in a sequence of notes,
chants in the crowd, a difficult poem.

The ring lilts like a theme song,
turns back on itself, a loop.
Oh, which dreams to chase?
Snooze wisely, my friend.

In the Jungle

My name appeared twice in the mock drafts,
both times in the high seventies
but after fourteen rounds and still no call
I could tell the margin was closing.
Then Owen Sound took the kid from Tecumseh
and I knew it was over.

No one else needed a goalie.

Coach shook his head, A damn shame.
Teammates denounced the league, Fuck the O.
And besides, Junior still left you eligible
for a scholly in the States.

I was taken early by Brockville,
too far to commute from home.
I billeted with a family in Tincap.

After practice, cheap beers from across the river,
grown men with unshaved cocks and hairy stomachs
packing dips, lippers, dingers, chompers.

The speed stagnated but pucks came quicker,
a game more rugged than graceful. I got bumped
by a guy in Smiths Falls and watched Zimmer retaliate,
got tossed like a rag doll but what choice did he have?
Someone hits the goalie.

Kessler in the sin bin, fuming, missing his time
like a dog behind glass.
He came out barking, cross-checked the first yellow jersey—
a fifteen-year-old colt fresh out of Midget,
thinking his pride on the line, slashes him back.

Next thing you know the gloves are off, the kid's lying on the ice
and there's an eerie silence between the screams.

Refs should've called it.
The rook being carted off,
both benches banging their sticks,
Kessler hammering the boards from the box.
All the scoresheet said was technical, five for fighting,
nothing about the rule he had broken.

It was me they went for—
vulnerable nestling, alone in the net.
Slew foots, extra hacks after the whistle
and the refs letting it all go,
atoning for what they couldn't punish.

My second game in the jungle and I somehow
make it through, with a win, nonetheless.

Threats from the lobby,
rink rats shouting for vengeance.
See you in February, Kessel.
Your goalie's gotta month to hit puberty.

Last to leave the rink,
I fasten the buttons on my collared shirt,
slip the tie over my head and pull it tight,
like a noose.

Late-Game Surge

So one of their guys, that duster with the nasty lip lettuce, fires a muffin down the ice. Masser's off in his own world, probably eyeing one of the broads in the stands, and he barely gets a piece of it. The biscuit bounces off one of his pillows and into the corner. I'm the first one back, so naturally I scoop it and start looking for an outlet. Banksy's supposed to be posted by the hashmarks but he's already calling for a change 'cause his lungs are gassed. All I see—three green tarps flying towards me like the Vietcong. The whole barn is buzzing 'cause Abrams is leading the charge and they think he's looking for a tilly. Buddy spends the entire game chirping but when it's time to go, those gloves stay glued to his fucking hands. Anyway, Abrams is flying in, lookin' to throw the bow, so I fake a pass up the boards, put the rubber between his legs, make him look like the pigeon he is. After that I just go for a rip. I wheel past O'Hara and that bender with the birdcage, then sauce a pass to Gibbsy. Gibbsy turns on the jets, dangles some pylon out of his fucking jockstrap, then drops it back. I start looking for someone to feed it to. That's when the crowd goes silent and I realize I'm all alone on the point. Coop's in front of the pipes, screening the tendy. He's giving me this look that says, Shoot the fucking thing already. So I decide to just tee it up. A clap-bomb. The goaler drops to his knees 'cause Coop's giving him the business. The puck goes right over the kid's shoulder. Pings off the iron, bar south. The zebra flies in like somebody's been stabbed, throws his arm down. Then the lamp starts flashing. That's when I realize I actually potted a gino. The celly? Shit, I don't know. It's not every day your boy tickles the twine like that. Guess I was just happy it wasn't greasy. Fuckin' eh, boys. A dub's a dub.

Skate Like 6 / Rowe-try

You see it on the court. Player dancing
the ball on a rope. Clean snap of the net.

Or the gridiron. Toes teasing the sideline.
Pigskin corralled into outstretched fingers.

Baseball has its diamond. Flying fielders
nabbing the end of the arc. The poetry of sport.

No one ever called the arena a graceful place.
Too brutal. Too bloody.

But there's a beauty in this game
embedded in all the mayhem.

We saw it first in Keegan, the way he skated,
the puck trailing his stick like a shadow.

Or the kid from Brockville in his early days,
flowing through bodies like water.

Twelve years old and we saw their grace for what it was,
a mastery we would never achieve.

A thousand wind-sprints, a hundred summers at camp,
something told us we would never skate like Six.

We learned to root for contact, the guy who dropped the mitts.
Fifteen dirty dogs. A lone cat.

Our game changed. New crowd favourites.
New heroes.

Effort, tenacity, grit.
These were the moves of mortals.

But when Six touched the puck, sheesh,
you didn't dare turn away.

You just held your breath, stared, and prepared to witness
the chance of something divine.

Midnight in Canmore

A cold cradle
rocks the mountains to sleep.

Barrelling trains
from the Canadian Pacific

haul Monday's freight
alongside murmurs of chinooks.

The heavy clamour of weathered metal
like a shiver through the nestled town.

Awake and stirring in a billeted bed
while the mountains sleep through.

Because nothing,
not even shrieking winds,

can break their heavy slumber.

When Last I Left

When last I left this town
the trail was trampled
by the nine to fivers.

The boys had claimed the booth
beneath the speaker and Hodgey
had chosen to pour.

Fernbank was under construction,
a telltale sign of changes to come;
Dirty Harry's had plans to expand.

But when I returned
years later to that same night
I noticed nothing.

A body will do that, regenerate
so subtly even the beholder
won't perceive of the shift.

A part of me is always there
in the warmth of that pub,
casually scrutinizing Hodge's surgeon focus
waiting to bombard his willingness
to take the reins.

We'll stomach success in silence,
pounce on flaw like a lame fawn.
A light glass, too much head,
the margin for error
has thinned over the seasons.
You learn to take only the shots
you think you can make.

But what kind of man
withholds praise
from those closest to him?
As though it were finite, a pitcher's worth,
when all we have in this world
is a single glass to our name.

I think it's time
for me to leave the arena,
step far away, polish my stroke
in foreign lands and forget
about the blood in the sand.

The trail has frozen
from too many steps.

Only dogs deviate
from the path.

Welcome to Deutschland

Coach met me at the airport holding a sign
with a maple leaf. My goalie bag jammed the x-ray.
Offsetting omens.
Velcome to Deutschland, he said, grabbing my sticks.
The team is excited to meet you.

Dressing room, a few hours before puck drop, opening night.
Guys are wary, but they shake my hand anyway,
sneak glances when they think I'm not looking,
try to determine if I'm *the guy*.

Rink like a sprinkled donut, hole within.
From the tunnel, I survey what I can.
Drums, chants, a primitive energy.
Let's go, goalie. One of the guys, still nameless, taps my pads.
You ready?
I look to the crowd for an answer. He seems to get it.
Best to ignore them. They're going to expect a lot.
He nods at the truth of his own words.
Then, almost as an afterthought.
Love you or hate you, there's no in between.
What to do but nod.

Warm-up is a ritual, familiar as a shower routine.
Body on cruise control. Mind through the windshield.

The ice feels different, softer. Ads everywhere.
Fans already bouncing, waving flags like bedsheets.
The steady cadence of an unseen drum
keeping pace with my throated heart.

I take a line of shots, back then forth.
Fresh off the plane this morning, I feel stiff, bloated,
but best to steer black thoughts to the corners.

First few minutes are a jam—gridlock in the neutral zone.
One of their guys picks up the biscuit, fires it down the ice.
I leave my crease to play it, but the boards here are different.
A weird bounce, next thing you know the puck's in the net
and we're down by one.

The air in the building gone, just like that.

One of my D-men, Big Bjorn, glides over shaking his head.
Unlucky. You get the next one.
I scoop the puck from the net, look to the crowd.
A thousand-eyed beast. Staring back. Unblinking.

The clock ticks on. I make some saves
but another gets by me, a screen the fans don't see.
Had it been the first, they might've let it slide.
As it is, I'm playing on thin ice. We're down two-zip
and I can feel the ice shrinking. The glass pressing in.

I look to our bench, see two players exchange a glance,
something in me sinks.

The crowd cares less for subtlety.
Taunts hurled over the boards.
Foreign words, but a smirk speaks
volumes in any language.

The noise is pulling me under.
unwinding me strand by strand.
Birds squawk from above.

I'm about to submit to the pull,
inhale a lungful of water
when I see a jersey in my periphery.
Big Bjorn again, gliding in.
I sweep an arc of snow with my stick.
He waits till I meet his gaze. *Bruder*, he says.

There's an honesty in his eyes, something pleading and real.
We know what you can do. Relax.
A tap on the pads—enough to buoy the drowning.

We pot two in the second. The third, scoreless.
I'm standing on my head but I won't dare look up.

Overtime's a deadlock, boxers exchanging blows.
When the horn finally sounds, the scoreboard reads tie.

For the first time in forty minutes, I allow myself
a glance at the clock.
The zeroes like a single pair of eyes, surveying.

It isn't hard to infer what's to come.
The fans are buzzing.
There's an electricity in the air, something palpable.
Too much excitement for more overtime.
Realization dawns on me.
Like a desperado, that word I love and dread so much:

Shootout.

They don't flood the ice. No added suspense.

All eyes on our bench, waiting to see who gets the nod.
Perilli hops the boards. Another Canadian,
another import, with stakes just as high as mine.
The crowd claps, more curious than hopeful.

Perilli takes his time skating in.
There's a poise in his stride, something to distrust.
He cradles the puck to some internal rhythm,
biding his time in a game of chicken.
He's in close, and I almost fret, but their goalie bites—
big mistake—tries to poke check.
Perilli pulls it from the flailing stick

like a broom on hardwood,
rolls to the backhand and tucks the puck
over the goalie's shoulder.
The red light flashes—pause—then the cheer.
Like a discharge.
Perilli curls around and punches the sky.
The gesture speaks volumes, shakes the monkey
right off his back.

One play, a fraction of a second,
and he's won them all over.
Big moments like these solidify reputations,
or destroy them.

I know where I stand. A solid two periods, no doubt,
but in this situation, anything short of a win is a loss.
They start with their import,
tit for tat, a Yank from one of the Big Ten schools.
A defenseman, not known for finesse,
but his team is calling for favours.
Imports do important things in important moments.

I almost feel sorry for him, the way he scoops the puck.
He's telling me something.
A single trick in his bag, he isn't one to read the room.
It goes against every lesson—the goalie must outwait
the shooter—I lunge.
If I'm wrong, I'm gone. Face-down, looking like a fool.
But he panics, fires a shot into my chest. *Nein*, the ref shouts.
The bench bangs their sticks.
Murmurs from the crowd.

I pang the posts, bend over, and plan to go inward,
but cheers draw my attention.

I look up and see Müller skating to centre,
the crowd on their feet.
I don't yet know my teammates, but I know Müller.
He's the guy on the programs, the billboards, the posts on IG.
Team Captain for the last six years.
A local product. The heart and soul.

It's moments like these that will solidify Müller's legacy,
a point he knows too well.
I watch him bend and test the flex on his stick.
The crowd, the team, you can see they're rooting for him.
They want him to be the guy they think he is.
Müller seems detached from it all.

The ref's whistle pierces the clamour.
A collective inhale. Silence.
Then sound—Müller's blades carving their way up the ice.
He's skating faster than Perilli, weaving
back and forth like a high-frequency wave,
scouting the net, trying to lose the goalie
in a game of angles.
I watch him with detachment, admiration. I want to call
the boys back home, tell them
these Euro players have tricks like you wouldn't believe.
Müller pumps, lifts a skate, then stops suddenly. The goalie
slides, and Müller, the crafty bastard, pulls it back,
tucks the puck between the tendy's legs.
The ref drops an arm. The crowd erupts.
Danke schön, Captain.

Their final shooter, the guy who potted the first one,
a dirty dangler from the eastern block, surveys me, not the ref.
When the whistle chirps, he scoops the puck, starts skating.
Fast.
I distrust the speed.
His visor like a hat brim, cocked on his head.
He's got something up his sleeve,
we can all see that.

I run through what I know I know.
Match his speed. Follow the puck, not the body. Be patient.
Be patient.
Be patient.

He's in close. I realize
he's waiting for a lunge that won't come.
Every passing nano-second
leaving him deeper in the hole he's digging.
I'm in sync with the puck, I've got the net.

He dipsy-doodles; I stay locked.
Pulls it to his backhand but I'm there.
Tries one last fake, finds a wall.
A desperation flick; I flash the leather.
The ref swings his arms out—*I love you this much*.
The team's already off the bench, the crowd hopping.

Big Bjorn the first to greet me.
Atta be kid. Welcome to Deutschland.

After teammates have cleared, I peek to the crowd,
on its feet, clapping. No longer a beast. I see
individual faces, people
as fickle and flawed as me.

Roma

Dropped toppings
between the cobblestones,

a poppy-print skirt, white blouse,
a smile that could melt butter.

Behind glass, a sunbaked tabby
tracking geckos
along ancient walls
       time-soaked by the same sun.

La fontanella pours cold
water into the heated streets.
Il nasone, she calls it, the big nose.
She love-taps my bridge, traces a line to the lips.
Nasone. Her smile the opposite of a bad intention.
She's too soft for her words to cause harm. It's too hot.

Reality is something distant;
the doubt remote.

We binge on eye contact, soft-tongued kisses,
let our hands
grow sweaty in constant embrace.

To acknowledge the moment would be futile.
In forty-eight hours, we'll be forced to return,
strangers once again
in different cities.

Bus Ride

I'm more seasoned to these long rides than the Europeans.
My country is big, I tell teammates, *we're conditioned to travel*.
But eighteen hours. Vejle to Vienna. Men were broken
over less.

The embarkment, a ceremony. Wives and girlfriends
sending off sailors with bagged lunches and neck pillows
to waters fraught with Tinder sirens.
Anna und Olga singing through screened shores.
The fluency of emojis. Communication without words.

The bus pulls out of the lot as we wave goodbye.
Niko catches sight of his car, his phone on the dashboard.
Four letters. Four-fifths of a second. One word.
Then, just as quickly, he accepts his fate. *Meh, I'll be fine.*

Thirty-six hours plus change. A long way to travel
with one's own thoughts.

*

On the road ahead   the road ahead
our eyes are locked   on the road ahead
where the changing of lines   from solid
to free   becomes something of a ceremony.

*

Forehead pressed against the vibrating glass
just to feel
something.

*

My knees are locked. So is the bathroom door.
A beautiful shame. My only reason to stand.

I remember bus seats being bigger, or maybe we were
just smaller,
and something other than obligation awaiting our arrival.
Ministicks, a hotel pool, manhunt. Little chocolates
on the pillows.
Pleasures were hiccups in routine.
Nice ones.

*

The bus carries the energy of garbage.
Not bag blowing in the wind garbage.
But landfill garbage. Garbage absolute.

I want to tell the boys what we did
on these long journeys to kill time
but for the life of me, I cannot recall.

I remember DVDs voted upon.
Parents playing gin, drinking rummy.
A tangle of shared headphones.
The lone hall like a catwalk for hockey moms
padding their awkward paths to the shitter.

Doug's mom heard him say shitter
and then took away his Nano. Doug
turned inward. Now he's an architect.
Bingo's Dad stunk up the bathroom
and now Bingo lives with his mom.

For some of us—Meter, Rasmus, Scoob—this ride
is one big set. Social creatures, they relish an audience.
Meter's the Prince of Denmark, delivering a soliloquy
to a crowd of three or four.
I'm lost in the lilt of his cadence. We all are.

When the punch line comes—and even I can tell
—the bus cracks up.

I watch a smile linger on Theis' face then slowly disappear.
And in that instant the answer dawns on me.
The trick to these long rides.

I'm about to turn and tell the boys I have the answer
but something stops me.
A shift in the light, perhaps, a passing cloud
and the moment no longer seems right.

*

Dust motes cling to the other side of the window.
Outside, a rolling field of canola, mango yellow.
Blue skies with a tiny bump on the horizon.
Eyes locked on what lies ahead. Psalm of the open road.
Because even flat land will at some point rise.

Words That Need to Surface

Bus ride home from Copenhagen,
the guys celebrating. I sit up front
where it's easier to decline drinks.
Henrik has his eye on me. I feel
his gaze. He's worried about the hit.
I didn't tell him about the blurring,
the yellow hue the rink took. I called
it a stinger, shooed him off the ice.
Back home, I swallow some omegas,
a handful of dried cranberries
to reduce inflammation, walk
twice around the neighbourhood.
Exercise stimulates blood flow to the brain.
I'm climbing our street when I get
her text. *Excited to see u tonight :)*
I stop at the edge of the driveway.
Our house like a ship in the night.
In the warm glow of the kitchen
I see the boys drinking, shouting,
celebrating the win. Quiet's discord.
Something in me balks. On a whim
I turn around and walk downtown,
let myself into the gym with a key.
Biking, stretching, a light pump.
Good to stimulate blood flow to the brain.
My mistake is going to her place after.
I make popcorn, douse it in olive oil,
leave it for when she returns, drunk,
stumbling. I try feigning sleep but
she has words that need to surface.
I dressed up for you tonight, she says.
Her 'r's harder, her voice a cocktail
of anger and pain. I mumble a sorry
but she isn't finished. Her wounds

are deep, my flesh in plain sight.
Your boys were mad too, all talking shit.
I bite the line and like a fish, regret it.
What were they saying? I sit up in bed.
A smile. She knows I'm snagged.
She takes her time dropping her bag.
Maybe tonight she can return
some of the pain I've caused her.
Maybe she's as fucked up as I am.
Maybe I don't care.
Maybe I do.

Summer of '21

I woke up to sunlight,
lazy beams melting
like coco oil in my coffee.
On a couch that swallowed
coins, I put my feet up
and prayed for change—
a library book forever
within arm's reach.
I sang like cicadas,
shuffled songs by rappers
and cowboys, grown men
with smoky voices and
unfettered stories. At the
gym, I pushed two plates,
guzzled shakes, and snuck
glances at myself in the
mirror. I made bets and
threw frisbees, tongue-
kissed girls from foreign
cities, and took long late
night drinks from the sink.
I arced ping pong balls into
party cups, Kobe'd cans from
deep, and wind-mill dunked
on the mini-net. I swapped
stories and T-shirts, skipped
stones for clout, and learned
how to cut my own hair. I
stretched on the carpet, peed
in the shower, and conjured
a life for the future. Mornings,

I woke up to sunlight, chirps
from small birds, and sunk back
into my pillow, blissfully unaware
that these were my best days.

Dear Rookie

For 5

I'm going to try to be as honest as I can with this letter. At first,
   I didn't like you.
We met at the airport. Do you remember what you said?

Oh, so you're the goalie? I'm going to put so many past you.

In time I would learn that that was who you were. There was a
   level of playfulness to these bold statements – you would've
   said the same thing to Lundqvist—also a sense of sincerity.
   You believed in competition, in cultivating the best version
   of you. In doing so, you raised the standard of us.

We competed. In everything. Shooting pistachio shells into cof-
   fee mugs, guessing which subway would arrive first, throw-
   ing stones into blossoming ripples.
At practice, every puck counted. When I saw you skating up the
   ice, I found my second gear.

Most times, I won. I had the finesse and focus you didn't, sea-
   soned traits. But I learned from you. Did I ever tell you
   that? I learned something crucial.
Because no matter the situation, the opponent or the score, you
   always lifted your fists.

In your eyes, opportunities were chances to improve your stock.
The time you dropped the mitts with Lindelof in practice.
Beaking while he pummelled you with punches.
I remember someone saying: *He's an idiot for fighting a teammate.
But he's got some dog in him.*

Do you remember the time we were at the field in Södermalm
   and decided to race?

We'd been jawing about who was faster since you arrived, and
finally agreed to settle it.

A man smoking a joint volunteered to arbitrate, and I'm glad he did.
Because the race was close.
So close. And I know both of us would've clung to that thin
sliver of subjectivity.

Before we lined up, you asked that we keep the result private.
To date, only three people know who won that race.
Me, you, and the man with the joint.

Ayo, take my picture. This was one of your favourite lines.

I'd be in my room, reading, and you'd barge in wearing a new
sweater, or a shirt I'd never seen.
You'd strike pose after pose and I'd envy you.
For all the fire in your soul. For all the shine.

Girls loved you. You knew how to be charming.
I would sometimes listen to the things you told them, and
smile. You knew the secret lay in your authenticity.
You fanned those flames until fires raged.
And then wondered why people got burned.

Do you remember the time we caught the rat in our apartment?
I was the one who said we had to kill it, lest it find its way back.
As we proposed different methods, I noticed you growing uneasy.
When the water bucket came out, you finally snapped.
It has a soul, you know?

One day, while walking to the subway, I wanted to listen to
music. I picked a song by Wale. But when I put the phone
in my pocket, my finger tapped another track, *Don't It* by
Billy Currington. Unflustered, I scrolled back to Wale. But
when I went to return the phone to my pocket, I tapped the
screen again. *Don't It* started playing. Again.

I would relay this story to you and Keanu at dinner that night.
Keanu called it a coincidence. You called it a sign.

I loved the way you asked questions. Openly, unguardedly, with
a genuine yearning for truth.
My favourite question of yours: We were in the living room,
talking about our apartment's mouse and ant problem,
when you cleared your throat:
Do mice eat ants? you asked. There was a hesitation in your
voice, a reluctance. *Do mice. Eat. Ants?*
It was subtle but detectable. We all burst out laughing. And I
watched your heart sink.
I replay that scene a lot.
Conjure up the million other ways I could've responded.

My phone is filled with photos of you. My favourite is one I
captured on the subway.
Graffiti surrounding your head like a gloriole. You, a modern
Christ in a black hoodie, staring
into the abyss.
I wanted to photograph the water, but at the last second, the
train pulled into a tunnel, turning your window into a
black mirror.

What that photograph captures is depth. You're lost in some
internal world, dreaming up the big plays, the man you
want to be.
I'd never seen those eyes head on. It was the reflection that re-
vealed them. Like an eclipse. Gaze potent, like the sun.
Filled with fire.

The day I bought my camera. We brought it home and I
snapped pictures of you dunking on the mini-net.
At one point in the shoot, you got so excited you ripped off
your shirt.
This anecdote doesn't have a moral, a punchline. It just embod-
ies the essence of you.

We travelled out west, to Macke's cottage in Gothenburg, and you brought some drama with you. Something with a girl. With you, there was always something with a girl.

Shining sun, blue waters, birds wheeling overhead, all while you shouted into your phone, your emotions untethered. I lifted my camera and took two pictures. In the first, you look mildly offended, as though I had barged in on a personal moment. In the second, a sense of levity, your chin to the sky. Oh, how you loved to be photographed.

You'd miss one-timers in practice, or get beat along the boards, and the whole team would jeer.
They knew they could get a rise. But the Uppsala game at home, when you went end to end in the final minute and scored, the bench erupted like it was game seven. When push came to shove, everyone rooted for you.

Here's something you seem not to know: Others are capable of failure; you do not hold the patent.

They say the eyes are windows to the soul. Well, my friend, you are a house in the night, with every room aglow. You just happen to live in a world of drawn curtains. With nothing but darkness outside, all you end up seeing in that light is your own mess.

I envy your candour.
In a world full of masks,
you jut your chin to the sky,
and let your face shine.

You haven't even realized you're the hero.
May your story be great.

Rubber or Pieces

Sometimes I forget I'm not at home.
Winters in Sweden no different than
Ontario's mean. Snow falls the same.

Lazy sun. The early onset of night.
And the English. Properly spoken.
Better than my boys from back home.

But then I'll round a corner and feel space.
Lift my gaze from the stones and see blue.
Ice cubes jingling in drinks. Skolling sirens.

A saver to wade in this city of islands.
Where water can sustain or drown you.
Depending on how it is swallowed.

Sometimes I forget I'm not at home.
The water calms and I see my reflection.
An expression I tried to leave behind.

All these struggles. These wins.
What's the point if who we are
is as fixed as the sun, moon, and stars.

Maybe man is who he is. Irrevocably.
His pendulum swings but momentum
will settle. Leaving him back where he began.

I think that I'm sinking.
Like a watch in the ocean.
Straying further and further from light.

I pray that I'm rubber.
Fabricated for impact.
Flexed and destined to soar.

I think it's time to stop fighting the draft.
Rubber or pieces. I must submit to the fall.
Impact the ground. Find out what I am.

Jupiter Is Made of Stardust

We're out on the roof and for once the city lights
aren't swallowing up the night. You spot a star, low
on the horizon, and make your wish. I inch forward.
I can sense the question before you ask it.

Where are we headed?

The night sky is full of possibility but it lacks answers.
The stars that make up constellations are really light-years
apart. City lights have stolen our jewels of the night.
The moon like our last dangling ornament, a bulb of glass.

We've been here before. Not you and I. But a girl like you.
Four, five dates in and that frantic love I showered finally
starting to taper. And just as you begin to bloom. Cruel.

I'm learning to use my words. To breathe life into feeling.
Words are easy to weave into poems, but beneath all this night,
they die in my throat. The sky is a vacuum. There's a silence
between stars.

Did you know that space is incredibly clear? Light travels for years
unobstructed, just to bend at our door. The reason stars twinkle.

Also, Jupiter is made of stardust. It just never grew large enough
to ignite. You occupy yourself with that same wishing star while I
bite my tongue. Language is a force brewing. The fusion of words.

Most of my sentences start with Okay, and tend to leave
people silent. Stars shine in the day but nobody sees them.
That bright light you see low on the horizon isn't really a star.
It's a planet. More often than not, that first star wished upon
is actually its own little world.

Other Planets

It's funny how rarely I acknowledge the crowd.
I sense its presence, a forest of bodies, but it's something removed,
like the rise and fall of one's own breath.

My interest in this game is stable—
like earth as it orbits the sun.

*

I used to believe in a geocentric universe.
Stars were stars, and distant.

Sun was life. Hockey, my world.

A dichotomy. A constant dancing embrace.

*

I've been searching the sky with questions
and found answers in dawn and dusk.

Venus, Mars, Jupiter, and Saturn. Other planets.
They're there once you know where to look.

Once you know where to look, they're all you see.

*

My interest in this game is perfect. Perspective has sedated
my nerves.

Like an epiphany, an unshackling freedom, I've learned
a great truth.
Other planets orbit my sun. I see them on the horizon.

I'm still on Earth, but my time here is fleeting.

Soon I will wave goodbye, board a ship,
dip my toes in the sky and explore—

worlds and worlds beyond.

The Old Barn

The road takes me back, as it so often does,
to where it began.

I signal into the lot and see the building,
the orange and white stripes, the hackneyed font,
ugly and cozy as ever.

I park the car by the softball diamond and lean back,
quiet the whoosh of the heater.
Snowflakes dock on the windshield, melt upon touch.

After a minute, the arena doors open and a man
walks out, followed by a boy dragging his gear.
The wheels on his bag aren't turning. Too much snow.

The man pops the trunk, wrestles the bag
while the boy brushes the windows clear.
Their routine is one without words.
A habit, a comfy and careless pattern.

More snowflakes fall from the sky
before disappearing into the whole.

Snow blankets the lot. The only blemish, a pair
of tracks, and the lines the boy's bag has left behind.
Pencil-thin and parallel, they form a path
to the arena doors, where a lone bulb glows butter.

I take my cue and cut the engine. Something about
the way the light slices through the flurries,
like a full-moon, a candle, a beacon for sailors,
or plagued man seeking answers.

I pull the glass door and warmth washes over me.
The sangria-red flooring, unchanged after all these years.
A network of skate marks,
like all the tiny creases in your palm.

The lobby is smaller than I remember.
The canteen gate is closed.
No sour shocks or five-cent Dubble Bubbles.
A thin light leaks with the hum of the cooler,
the gentle whirl of red and blue slush.

The dressing rooms are open, and again, what strikes me
is the size.
I can see sixteen boys lining the perimeter, taping, lacing,
pulling taut
lessons unspoken, and the unseen sweat in the air.

Trophy cases line the wall.
Gilded heroes with stoic faces
frozen in glorious stride.
The candy cart where we turned caribous
into gumballs, jawbreakers, chews.
And the water fountain, pressure like a garden hose,
glacier cold, tapped into God's own well.

I pull the door into the rink. Another temperature shift.
The insect buzz of spotlights.
Wooden beams and a corrugated metal roof.

Habit pulls my gaze groundward.

Glossy and grand, a body at rest.
Flawless lines, and molten puddles of light
pooling in the sheen.

High above the benches, listless banners, stained yellow
with time.
Squinting, I make out some of the names. The numbers.
Think of all the journeys that began here—
the banker's, the soldier's, the cook's—
and the surface that holds their stories.

Triumphs, gassers, wounds.
Bench brawls, and chippy finishes.

The ice bears all.

The buzzer sounds, players retire,
but the game's signature remains

until the Zamboni pulls out
and through a calculated and practiced path
it wipes the ice clean.

You've Been Spending Your Days

staring skyward.
Distant white lights—
a reminder of what your city life has charged.
Your knee is broken. Scarred. Forever misaligned.
Your back will continue to wake you, long into the night.
Yet still your tendons cling. Unwilling to let go.

There are so many stars in the night sky—
beaucoup d'etoiles dans le ciel de nuit.
One could slip away, forever, without notice.

Only a salt-shake of stars
will ever comprise something more.
Orion was a fearless hunter.
Polaris showed the northern world the way.
Cast to the biggest stage,
some lights were just destined to follow paths.

Most stars, when they die, will not explode.
Supernovas—those brilliant spectacles—are reserved
for giants.

Our sun will not expire with a bang. A flourish. A big hurrah.
Like a balloon cast to the corner, it will deflate, shrink
and wither to nothing,
a silent shrivel in the grave of growing space.

Grace is an exit at the top. Pre-descension.
Nothing sadder than a once-hero
losing ground on his former self.

You can always play pick-up. Men's league.

How to explain the tragedy of that statement. ·
No. When you step away from this game, it will be for good.
You'll pack your bag one last time, zip it shut, and submit
to gravity, to collapse,
to dissolve,
and to the ever-expanding emptiness.

It's funny.
Looking back, the games, the saves, they've all but disappeared.
Blended into something just beyond my reach.
My time on that ice, like ice everywhere, was transient.
Destined to melt.
What's lingered, what continues to greet me,
are those skateless moments.
Bus rides and backseats. Benches and bleachers. Hotel hallways.
The road.
Yes, I was a sun. But not because I withered.
Not because I was one of many.
I was a sun because, for a brief period in time,
I shined. I radiated—
In my cosmic moment, I gave life to an entire world.

Four Captains

4 — My best friend. Not an ounce of salt when they gave you the C. Not the loudest in the dressing room, or the largest, but something about the way you approached the game—calmly, strategically—inspired a world of confidence. You carried the poise of a large stone. Scanned the ice like a chessboard. Head up, and on a swivel. Facilitating. In a time of wicked, open-faced blades, shots that panged glass, you opted for subtlety. The P96 Bouchard. An Easton Modano. The closed-face curve easier for keeping pucks on the ice. At a time when everyone aimed for crossbars, you, four, searched methodically, mercilessly for your teammates' sticks.

20 — In describing great leaders, language often falls short. What a true leader embodies is bigger than words. You weren't a formula or a recipe, a puzzle to deconstruct. You were the whole. Unapologetically imperfect. Effortlessly suave. You saw a path through the brambles. And like a shepherd, you plotted to show us the way.

9 — You embodied hockey. The skill, the guts, the grit. I watched you dance through defenses, body big men, and heave your frame in front of flying pucks. Mr. Everything. The player you came to watch. And yet, talent wasn't your ace. What you played for was unmistakably clear. Do you remember that game in Orleans? The dogfight, chippy from the get-go. We were on a penalty kill when the brawl broke out. I saw a free man and left my crease. More of an attack than a tilt, it lasted less than ten seconds. The ref grabbed me, hollered for the whole rink to hear: *The goalie's outta here.* Leaving the ice, one of their guys speared me in the back of the knee. It was subtle but you caught sight of it, dropped the gloves again, your second scrap in two minutes. With the ref's arm on my shoulder, I watched you fight my fight, like a Pitbull. Like I said, what you played for, nine, was unmistakably clear.

23 — Accountability. That's what you brought to our team. You so clearly gave it your all, and success followed you like a shadow. I never told you this, but I once overheard you on the phone with your mom one night. You in the kitchen, me in my room. Your voice was muffled, but the house was quiet, and I heard every word. *They'll never understand the grind, Mum.* I never learned the context of that statement, or what prompted it. All I remember is the feeling, like a key being turned. Your secret revealed. Struggle. In your dogged pursuit of success, you were willing to outwork everyone. I never told you this either, but I idolized you. That semi-final game in Aalborg. You had four goals. The score tied. You in the dressing room before the third, crying, pleading. *It can't just be me.* It was the want in your voice. An import, and you cared more than all of us. We fought like dogs in the third. For you. It was always for you, twenty-three.

To the Vet

For 44

Routine solidified our friendship.

We'd wake early and pad around the hardwood
while the rest of the house slept.

You always prepared breakfast—eggs, Polar bread, dollops
of cream cheese, oatmeal, bananas—while I scooped
coconut oil and butter into our coffees.
If there was a theme to those autumn mornings, it was caloric intake.

We'd walk to the station in silence or speak in clipped sentences
subdued by the morning frost.
On the train, we sat next to strangers, the nine-to-fivers,
and failed to blend in.
Your sheer girth, ballcap, and sweats
like a blue passport stapled to your chest.

You still had your programs from the University of Wisconsin
and we followed them like zealots. Never deviating.
We talked as much as we needed to. Grinded instead.

Words were like screws, used sparingly, as needed.
Nice. Up. Go. Rarely polysyllabic.
Sweat was our currency. We paid the rubber.

A post pump sauna, too hot for comfort,
neither of us wanting to be the one to call it.
You outlifted me, so I polished my will in that heat.

After, we'd take that same subway back, and catch either the 6
or the 218, whichever came first.
As a game, we stared out the windows and searched for guys
who could *kick your ass.*

I had fun pointing out semi-fit men—road workers,
locos in short sleeves, grizzled bikers—then making firm stands
that they could beat you in a fight. You just laughed.

At the team restaurant, we'd pile food onto our plates,
testing the limits of surface area.
You'd mix everything together—slop, as you called it
—and I'd call you an animal.
All going to the same place, buddy.

We argued daily over how many napkins a given meal warranted.
You never once said more than two.
That might've told me something about the way you approached the day.

After your food was gone, you'd stand, wordlessly, and fetch us coffees.
I'd still be eating, and you took that time to open up.
You liked to talk.

Social Hercules, that's what I called you, for your ability
to captivate any crowd.
We were different in that sense.
People drained me. They seemed to enliven you.
Social banter was your caffeine.
So was coffee. Gone before I ever finished my meal.

At practice later, you'd hover around the net.
A stay-at-home defenseman, a goalie's best-friend.
With legs like tree-trunks, you plowed the crease clear.

Your hands and strides were choppy, but you had poise.
I never once saw someone knock you off the puck.

You potted goals on occasion, shin-high howitzers from the point,
but scoresheet aside, your value was unparalleled. You were the voice
our team needed. The general.
We all would've followed you into a foxhole.

Nights, we'd return to that same gym, but with less urgency.
Lulling around the mats, we'd stretch, roll, knead out nagging knots.
You'd hijack the speaker system and we'd listen to country albums.
Morgan Wallen, ZBB, Luke Combs.

We'd coast on the stationaries and sing softly,
like cowboys on a moonlit ride.

Now I'm dodging potholes in my sunburnt Silverado.

I don't think you ever felt self-conscious.
God never burdened you with an ego.

Like a heart broke desperado headed right back to my roots.

Here's something I never told you:
Sometimes, I felt like Tonto,
your supporting roll.

You were the sun, bright and lively. Worlds danced in your orbit.
I was the moon.
With no real light to shine, I was forced to borrow yours.

But those nights, on those bikes, I was able to squash my demons
and sing the way birds do, without a care to who listens.

We'd ride that long metro home,
and try our hand at pronouncing the stops.
The carts were always empty, but still we'd sit together.

Our final stop was the park near our house where we'd jump
feet first into the Baltic.

My favourite part was that split second between
hitting the water and the onslaught of cold.
When, for a fleeting moment, we had outrun feeling.

Surfacing, we'd swim frantically to the ladders,
climb two steps, and leave our legs submerged.

Our backgrounds warranted that we never complain about cold.
Not at length.

From ladder to ladder, we communicated.
I called Wisconsin winters soft, asked if you even got snow.
You said I travelled too much to still be considered Canadian.

It was easy to go inward, but longer that way, so we talked.

I taught you our national anthem in those icy waters.
You stumped me with Eastern European capitals.
Names like sirens. Beautiful sirens. Sofia. Riga. Tirana.

When that timer went, we coolly clambered up the ladder.
Like it was no big thing.

It was the walk home that did it for me.
A flood of endorphins, ache-free joints, a warm bed waiting.
The way the water seemed to sway,
lapping at stones painted with moonlight.
Lone bulbs from across the water revealing cottages
obscured by daytime foliage.

A wrapped towel, damp but drying.
The quiet between words. The comfort.
Those were the feelings I chased.

Coach for a Day

Listen to me brother.
I don't claim to be a wise man
but curiosity has imparted to me
a pocket full of lessons.

Don't be afraid to ask questions
but remember to leave a door as you found it.
Even the fool can share with you
if nothing but a fresh perspective.

Cupboards and dressers have drawers
for a reason. Organize your thoughts.
Befriend the stranger who smiles in passing.
These waters are lonely. It's good to know sailors.

Sometimes the bull shits as you pass the pasture.
Most times a banana in your backpack results in disaster.
The breeze that cools your neck on a summer's day
is the same breeze that chills your spine in the rain.

Don't blame the breeze. Don't blame the rain.
Attitude and effort are easy substitutes for skill.
Respect the man who tries to peel his orange
in one shot. A second set builds muscle, a third

builds character. Don't trod through fresh snow
when someone's footprints have formed a path.
The only thing riskier than a bad poem
is a good idea for one. The moon controls the tides.

We're all just made of water.

Home Again

I'm surprised at how easily
it all comes back.
First shot of the night, a floater
tracked effortlessly into the glove.

Muscle memory, huh?
I bob the cat-eyed cage
an easy acquiescence.
Guess so.

There isn't time to wrestle with truths.

The crouch has atrophied,
my butterfly nothing but an exoskeleton.
But a good captain can still pilot old wings.
This heart has pumped too many beats
beneath these ice-furred rafters to forget.

And the voice,
riding high when the puck stayed out,
falling mightily when I looked behind.
Each failure a digital tally
for everyone to gaze on.

High-highs, low-lows, a pattern destined
to follow me through life like a shade.
Position or disposition? Chicken or egg?

After the game, a 7-2 win, I down my beer,
hasten to unbuckle the straps and escape
before they can ask.

The rink resides in my memory—
alongside the scent of rubber mats,
the sound of pulled tape,
the cold ecstasy of arena water from a plastic bottle.

Standing prompts the question,
Can we call you next time we need a tendy?
From the shower, *Let's just get rid of Donny*
and sign his contract now.
Laughter, the familiar acoustics of the dressing room.
How does a two-four of Canadian sound?
Win bonus of a pint per person.
All I can do is shake my head. *Don't think so, boys.*
Why not?
A room full of eyes
awaiting an answer like puck-drop.
Because you can't go home again.
More laughter, my cue to exit.

Outside, snowflakes swarm the streetlights
before drowning in coffee-coloured puddles.
I bury my bag in the trunk and pull out,
not bothering with the rear-view.

A goalie's job is to keep it all in front of him.
No good ever came from looking behind.

Notes

The Church of Saturday Saints:
   - Cujo: a nickname given to Toronto Maple Leafs goaltender Curtis Joseph

At the Stittsville Dance:
   - Cha-cha real smooth: a line from Cha-Cha Slide by Mr C The Slide Man
   - Crank Dat: a song by Soulja Boy
   - Lean Back: a song by Fat Joe
   - Cotton Eye Joe: a song by Rednex
   - YMCA: a song by the Village People
   - Macarena: a song by Los Del Rio

L'entraineur:
   - The Rocket: a nickname given to Canadian hockey legend Maurice Richard
   - The Q: a nickname given to the Quebec Major Junior Hockey League
   - T-push: an explosive lateral movement used to cover large areas of the crease

Pont du Portage:
   - The O: a nickname given to the Ontario Hockey League

In the Jungle:
   - Dip: a pinch of chewing tobacco (see lipper, dinger, chomper)
   - Lipper: see dip
   - Dinger: see dip
   - Chomper: see dip
   - Someone hits the goalie: In hockey, it is seen as intentionally provocative to attack an opposing team's goalie
   - Sin bin: the penalty box
   - Slew foot: a move where a player – using his stick or skate – trips or sweeps the legs of their opponent from behind
   - The Jungle: a monicker often used when referring to Junior hockey

Late-Game Surge:

- Duster: a player who doesn't see a lot of ice time and collects dust on the bench
- Lettuce: hair
- Lip Lettuce: a moustache
- Muffin: a shot that lacks power and typically spans the length of the ice
- Biscuit: a puck
- Pillows: goalie pads
- Tarp: a jersey
- Barn: an arena
- Tilly: a fight
- Chirp: trash talk
- Pigeon: a player who picks up scraps from his linemates
- Bender: an untalented player whose ankles bend when they're skating
- Birdcage: a caged facemask
- Sauce: a smooth and well-executed pass or play
- Screen: a player obstructing a goalie's view of the puck
- Tendy: short for goaltender or goalie
- Clapper/Clap-bomb: a slap shot
- Zebra: a referee
- Lamp: red light behind the net
- Gino: a goal
- Celly: short for celebration
- Twine: mesh of the net

Rubber or Pieces:

- Skol: The Swedish word used for cheers

Four Captains:

- P96 Bouchard: Sher-wood P96 wooden hockey stick with a Pierre Marc Bouchard curve
- Easton Modano: An Easton hockey stick with a Mike Modano curve

To the Vet:

- Lyrics in this poem are from the song Sand in My Boots by Morgan Wallen
- Tonto: The Native American sidekick to the Lone Ranger.

Acknowledgements

A big thank you to the editors of the following journals, where these poems first appeared, some in different renditions:
The Antigonish Review: "Late-Game Surge"
EVENT: "Summer of '21"
filling Station: "In the Jungle"
The Literary Review of Canada: "Coach for a Day" (published as "Jr.")
Prairie Fire: "L'entraineur"; "Home Again"
Queen's Quarterly: "Jupiter Is Made of Stardust"; "Dear Rookie"
Yolk Literary: "Pont du Portage"

An early version of *Goalie* was longlisted for the 2020 CBC Poetry Prize.

Thank you to the Goulbourn Rams, La Courneuve Flash, Prague Black Panthers, Basel Gladiators, Stockholm Mean Machines, Triangle Razorbacks, Hildesheim Invaders, Murcia Cobras, and the Cape Town Storm. These poems would not have been possible without the players, coaches, management, and fans who comprise these teams.

Thank you to the four captains listed in the poem, "Four Captains." They are, in order of appearance, Chris McDonald (to whom this book is dedicated), Ryan Turner, Brad Barton, and Niko Lester. I have tremendous respect for all of you, and it was my privilege to try and transcribe some of your tremendous character into words.

Thank you to Ajax Olson, who painted the spectacular base for this cover, and who continues to surprise me with his kindness and generosity.

Thank you to the entire team at Guernica Editions, especially First Poets series editor, Elana Wolff, for her keen eye and attention to detail. Huge thanks to publishers Michael Mirolla and Connie McParland, and associate publisher Anna van Valkenburg, for believing in this book, and to publicist Crystal Fletcher. None of this would have been possible without you.

Thank you to my parents, who encouraged me to chase passions, and who gave me the freedom and the unwavering support to do so. And thank you to my sister who spurred me forward when I was tempted by other paths.

Lastly, thank you to you, the reader, for sitting down with my story and giving my words a place to land.

About the Author

Ben von Jagow is a Canadian writer, athlete, and photographer. Ben is a graduate of Western University. His work has appeared in *Amsterdam Quarterly*, *The Stockholm Review of Literature*, *Canadian Literature*, *Queen's Quarterly*, *Prairie Fire*, *EVENT*, and *The Literary Review of Canada*, among other publications. For more of Ben's work, visit benvj.com.